MW01182063

Willa Cather

American Novelist

Tammy Orr Staats

PEARSON

Boston, Massachusetts
Chandler, Arizona
Glenview, Illinois
Upper Saddle River, New Jersey

Illustrations
Opener, 1, 8, 9, 10, 12, 15 Mike Lacey; 7 Joe LeMonnier.

Photographs
Every effort has been made to secure permission and provide appropriate credit for photographic material.
The publisher deeply regrets any omission and pledges to correct errors called to its attention in subsequent editions.

Unless otherwise acknowledged, all photographs are the property of Pearson Education, Inc.

Photo locators denoted as follows: Top (T), Center (C), Bottom (B), Left (L), Right (R), Background (Bkgd)

2 Prints & Photographs Division, LC-USZ62-82912/Library of Congress; 3 An American Time Capsule, Rare Book and Special Collections Division, rbpe13401300/Library of Congress; 4 Jupiterimages/Thinkstock; 5 (Inset) Prints & Photographs Division, LC-DIG-ppmsca-08378/Library of Congress; 6 FSA/OWI Collection, Prints & Photographs Division, LC-USF34-008666-D/Library of Congress; 11 Prints & Photographs Division, LC-DIG-ppmsca-08375 /Library of Congress; 13 FSA/OWI Collection, Prints & Photographs Division, LC-USF33-001468-M3/Library of Congress.

ISBN-13: 978-0-328-67645-3
ISBN-10:   0-328-67645-4

3 4 5 6 7 8 9 10 VOFL 15 14 13 12

A Famous Writer

Willa Cather's life was an adventure. In 1883, her family left Virginia for a new life in the Midwest. They made the move along with thousands of other families of **pioneers**.

The Nebraska **prairie** where they moved didn't look like any place that Cather had ever seen before. This landscape was flat. There were tall grasses that stretched on forever. There were few roads and towns, but there *were* neighbors. Many were **immigrants** from other countries. Most of the pioneers had one thing in common. They had gone west hoping for a new and better life.

Cather became famous for writing about characters like the ones she had met in her childhood. Today, Willa Cather is considered one of America's great writers.

Early Years

The oldest of seven children, Willa Cather was born in Virginia in 1873. The family lived in the Shenendoah Valley in a house named Willow Shade.

Cather's uncle had recently moved to Nebraska. Many other people were moving west as well. Many had responded to advertisements and

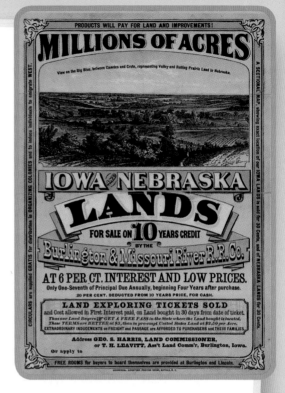

An advertisement for land

pamphlets. They had been promised land as well as happiness. Most had heard good things about the plains of the Midwest. Farming, they were told, would be easy there.

All this sounded appealing to Cather's father. A move west was interesting to him. A number of Cather's relatives had died of a disease called tuberculosis. Some people said that the prairie offered a healthier climate than Virginia.

The Big Move

In 1883, a fire destroyed the sheep barn at Willow Shade. The Cathers decided that now was the time to move. In the spring of 1883, nine-year-old Willa Cather, her parents, her three siblings, and several other family members made their way across the country by train. When they arrived at the train station in Red Cloud, Nebraska, a wagon and team of horses took them the sixteen miles to their new home.

Cather was startled by what she saw. Instead of the rolling hills and mountains of Virginia, she saw a flat, treeless landscape. Suddenly, Cather understood how someone could care about such things as woods, hills, and meadows. She felt as if she "had been jerked away from all of these things and thrown into a country as bare as a piece of sheet iron." She said, "As we drove further and further into the country, I felt . . . as if we had come to the end of everything."

The prairie was flat and treeless.

A New Life

At first, Cather felt lonely and homesick. The life of a Nebraska pioneer was not easy. The Cathers lived in a simple wood-framed house. Many others lived in simple houses made of blocks of **sod**. And, because many settlers had never farmed before, some farms failed.

Despite all this, Cather found herself starting to enjoy the vast open spaces that surrounded her. Cather was falling in love with the Nebraska prairie.

A typical house made of grass-covered dirt called sod

There were many one-room schoolhouses in the Midwest.

When in Virginia, Cather probably didn't hear many people speak a language other than English. In Nebraska, there were immigrants from many places, speaking many different languages. Cather attended school in a one-room schoolhouse, but her most valuable education came from spending time with the many immigrants she met. She came to appreciate and respect their **cultures**.

A Second Move

Less than a year after their arrival in Nebraska, Cather's father decided he was tired of farming. He moved his family to the town of Red Cloud and became a businessman.

Life in town was far different from life on the farm, 16 miles away. There was a little opera house in Red Cloud. Cather loved the music and shows she heard and saw there. She met an Englishman who offered to teach her to read Greek and Latin. A Jewish family allowed Cather to borrow from their large collection of books.

The Cather Family Homes

A Strong Personality

At the young age of 11, Cather got a job delivering mail. Every day she rode her horse from farm to farm with the mail. Along the way, Cather would stop and chat. The older immigrant women interested Cather. Later, Cather said, "I particularly liked the old women; they understood my homesickness and were kind to me."

Like many of those women, Cather had a strong personality. At the age of 15, Cather knew she wanted to be a doctor. At that time, there were few female doctors in the entire country. But Cather was determined. For a time, she cut her hair short, dressed like a man and called herself Wm. Cather, M.D. *Wm.* is an abbreviation for the name "William." She even went with some local doctors when they visited the sick.

The Cather family home in Red Cloud, Nebraska, still stands today.

The University of Nebraska

Becoming a Writer

Cather graduated from the one-room schoolhouse in 1890. She was asked to give the graduation speech. It was an honor to give the speech, and she was proud to give it.

At the age of 16, Cather left for the University of Nebraska in Lincoln. She still wanted to study medicine. But something happened that changed her plans. Without Cather's knowledge, an English professor submitted one of her **essays** to a local newspaper. Cather was thrilled when she learned that it had been published. Seeing her name in print made her change her career plans. Now, she realized, she wanted to become a writer. More than ever, she was determined to succeed.

After graduating from college, Cather returned to Red Cloud. Then she moved to Pennsylvania. For more than a decade, Cather made her living writing or editing for newspapers and national magazines. She also taught high school. However, by 1911, Cather began to focus solely on writing. And, in time, she began to write about what she knew best. That was the people and the places of the prairie.

Cather once said that the most important years in a writer's life are between ages eight and fifteen. These were the years in which people soaked up the world around them. They were also the years in which Cather lived in Nebraska. Cather started to write stories about the life and pioneer spirit of immigrants. Her writing felt real because she had seen it all firsthand.

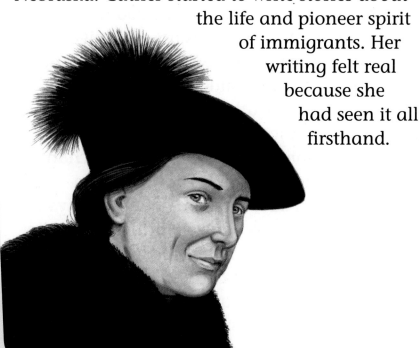

A pioneer family

O Pioneers!

Cather's first novel was not very successful. However, her second one, *O Pioneers!*, was a great success. It tells the story of Alexandra Bergman, the daughter of an immigrant from Norway who comes to Nebraska. Alexandra's father tries to farm but fails. He makes a request just before he dies. He asks his daughter to take over the farm.

Cather's father had once told her, "You have to show grit in a new country." Cather's character, Alexandra, has *grit*, another word for strength or courage. Alexandra has the toughness of the pioneers.

My Ántonia

Many people consider Cather's fourth novel, *My Ántonia,* to be her best. One character is a musician from Europe. Now he finds himself living in a sod house in the middle of the prairie. His family does not know the first thing about farming. However, this immigrant insists on dressing up in clothes from his home country. The story describes some of the difficulties that immigrants had adjusting to their new lives.

My Ántonia was published in 1918.

MY ÁNTONIA
BY
WILLA S. CATHER

Cather's Writing

Cather's characters, just like Cather herself, have a powerful connection to the land on which they live. Cather wrote about this. "There was nothing but land; not a country at all, but the material of which countries are made."

Cather's writing was unusual for the time. Her stories were moving but the language was plain. It was straightforward just as the lives of her characters were. Telling the stories of these pioneers was Cather's great gift to her readers.

As each book was published, Cather became better known as a **novelist**. In 1922, Cather won one of the most important prizes in America. She won the Pulitzer Prize for her fifth novel, *One of Ours*. The Pulitzer is one of the highest honors a writer can receive.

A Long Career

From time to time, Cather returned to Red Cloud. When she did, she always visited her old friends. She would also send them gifts during the holidays. During hard times, she sent them money and clothes.

Willa Cather had a long and successful career as a writer. She wrote essays, poems, short stories, and twelve novels. She also traveled around the country giving speeches. She became friends with many other respected writers.

Timeline of Willa Cather's Life

1873
Cather is born in Virginia.

1884
Cather's family moves to the town of Red Cloud.

1913
Cather publishes *O Pioneers!*

1870   **1880**   **1890**   **1900**

1883
Cather's family moves to a farm in Nebraska.

1891
Cather begins to attend University of Nebraska.

Willa Cather died on April 24, 1947, in New York City. As a famous writer, she had visited many places. But no matter where she went, Cather never forgot the vast, grassy prairie that had once been her home.

1922
Cather wins the Pulitzer Prize.

1920   1930   1940   1950

1918
Cather publishes
My Antonia.

1947
Cather dies in
New York City.

Glossary

culture the way of life of a group of people

essay a short piece of nonfiction writing on a specific topic

immigrant a person who moves to a new country

novel a long fictional story by a writer

novelist a person who writes novels

pioneer someone who is among the first people to settle in an area

prairie a large, mostly flat, area of grassland without trees

sod soil covered with thick grass